Non-Fiction
Teaching Notes

Gillian Howell

OXFORD
UNIVERSITY PRESS

Contents

Introduction

TreeTops Non-Fiction is an exciting extension to the TreeTops range. All the titles have been chosen to appeal to 7–11 year olds and have an appropriate reading ability level at their particular Stage. TreeTops Stages follow on from the *Oxford Reading Tree* stages, and are designed to be used flexibly with your individual pupil's reading ability. The levelling guide on page 5 gives you an indication of how the Stages correspond to the Year and age of the average pupil, together with the relevant match from the National Curriculum Level or Scottish, Northern Irish and Welsh equivalents.

Each book includes a Contents page, an Index and/or a Glossary of specialist terms or equivalent. These features enable teachers to develop children's information retrieval skills. In addition features of non-fiction texts, such as sub-headings, text boxes, and captions help children learn to skim-read a text for information. The series aims to fascinate children with surprising and interesting information.

How to introduce the books

Before reading the book, always read the title and talk about the possible content. Encourage the children to articulate what they already know about the subject, what they would like to find out and how they will use this book to do it. Complete the reading session with the pupils telling you what they have learned.

This booklet provides suggestions for using the book with groups of pupils or individuals. Suggestions are also provided for speaking and listening, further reading activities, ICT links and writing. These may be used as a follow on to the reading or used at another time.

Guided Reading Cards with built-in comprehension are available for each book. These provide detailed guidance for using the book for guided reading. Parental notes are included with each individual book.

Cross-curricular links with QCA/NLS objectives

Title	QCA Cross-curricular links	NLS objectives
Wall Soldier	History 6A A Roman Case Study	Y3T1 T17 understand the difference between fiction and non-fiction T19 locate information Y3T2 T14 how written instructions are organised
A-Z of Survival	Geography 7 Weather around the world	Y3T1 T18 notice differences in style and structure of fiction and non-fiction writing Y3 T2 T17 make notes
Tower of London	History 6B An Anglo-Saxon case study	Y3T1 T19 locate information T21 read information passages and locate main points Y3T2 T16 write instructions
Cutters and Crushers	Science 3A Teeth and eating	Y3T1 W13 collect new words form reading T19 locate information T22 make simple record of information from texts read
War Children	History 9 What was it like for children in the Second World War?	Y3T1T19 locate information T22 make simple record of information from texts read
Picture Dictionary of Ancient Egypt	History 10 What can we find out about Ancient Egypt?	Y3T1 T17 understand the difference between fiction and non-fiction T19 locate information Y3T2 T17 make notes

Levels Chart

Title	Treetops Tops Stage 11	NC level	Scotland	N Ireland	Wales
Wall Soldier	Year 3 terms 1 and 2 Age 7–8	Level 3	Level C	**Reading** Activities: a b f h i Outcomes: a b e g h k **Writing** Opportunities: b c d e Outcomes: b c e f g h i	**Reading** Range: 1 2 3 4 5 Skills: 1 2 3 5 6 7 8 9 Language development: 1 2 **Writing** Range: 1 4 5 Skills:1 2 3 5 6 Language development: 1 2 5 6
A-Z of Survival	Year 3 terms 1 and 2 Age 7–8	Level 3	Level C		
Tower of London	Year 3 terms 1 and 2 Age 7–8	Level 3	Level C		
Cutters and Crushers	Year 3 terms 1 and 2 Age 7–8	Level 3	Level C		
War Children	Year 3 terms 1 and 2 Age 7–8	Level 3	Level C		
Picture Dictionary of Ancient Egypt	Year 3 terms 1 and 2 Age 7–8	Level 3	Level C		

Wall Soldier

Reading the book with individuals and guided reading groups

Introducing the book

- Look together at the cover. Ask the children to suggest what sort of book this is, i.e. is it fiction or non-fiction?
- Ask them to look for clues on the cover that tell what type of book it is.
- Ask the children what they think they will find out by reading this book.
- Ask the children to name some of the typical features of non-fiction texts they expect top meet in this book, e.g. Contents page, Index, Glossary, photographs, captions, labels, diagrams.
- Ask the children to flick quickly through the pages and notice where they find any of these features.

Strategy Check

- Ask or remind the children about the strategies they can use to find specific information in non-fiction texts.
- Remind them about the strategies they can use to work out new words.

Focus of reading

- Explain that you want the children to find out one key piece of information for the following headings: equipment, food, entertainment, hygiene.
- Write the headings on the board as a reference for the children.

Independent reading

- Observe the strategies the children use when they meet new vocabulary, and prompt them as needed.
- Notice when the children use the Contents page to go straight to the chapters where they think the information they want will be found.
- Observe the children who scan the page to locate key facts.

Return and respond to the text

- Ask the children to say what key information they found for each of the headings on the board.
- Ask them to say how easy or difficult it was to identify their key facts.
- Ask other children to locate each other's key facts.
- Discuss which strategy helped them find the correct fact quickly, e.g. using the Contents page, flicking through the headings, scanning the page, etc.
- Ask the children to say how important the illustrations were in helping them locate and understand the information.

Further reading activities

- Ask the children to work with a partner, and to read pages 14 and 15.
- Ask them to play the game using the board on the following pages.
- Check that the children have read and understood the instructions.

Speaking and listening activities

- Ask the children to work in small groups of 3 or 4, and choose one chapter heading from the text.
- Ask them to discuss how to present this information to the class. Suggest they might mime it, or make it into a play, or give a factual presentation about the information.
- Ask some groups to perform it for the others.

ICT links

- Research further information on Roman Soldiers or Hadrian's Wall. The following website contains interesting and easily accessible information:
  http://museums.ncl.ac.uk/WALLNET

Writing

- Revise the features of Instruction texts.
- Ask the children to re-read pages 10 and 11, and write a set of instructions for making a sword.

A-Z of Survival

Reading the book with individuals and guided reading groups

Introducing the book

- Look together at the cover. Discuss the title. Ask the children what they understand by 'survival'. Ask the children to suggest what sort of book this is, i.e. is it fiction or non-fiction?
- Ask them to say how they think the information will be organised in this book.
- Encourage them to name some of the typical features of non-fiction texts, e.g. Contents page, Index, Glossary, photographs, captions, labels, diagrams.
- Ask the children to flick quickly through the pages and notice where they find any of these features. Discuss why an alphabetically organised text might not need an Index.

Strategy Check

- Ask or remind the children about the strategies they can use to find specific information in non-fiction texts.
- Remind them about the strategies they can use to work out new words.
- Ask the children to say where they would look in the text to find the meaning of a new word. Look together at the Glossary and read the words and definitions.

Focus of reading

- Ask the children to make notes of the things they should keep in a survival kit.
- Ask them to find out how the author convinces readers that he is an experienced 'survivor'.

Independent reading

- Ask the children to read the introduction, and then to scan the text to find the information about survival kits.
- Observe the strategies the children use when they meet new vocabulary, and prompt them as needed.
- Observe the children who scan the page to locate key facts.

Return and respond to the text

- Ask the children to say what they found out about survival kits. How easy or difficult was it to locate the information?
- Discuss the author's credentials from the introduction on page 4. Ask them to scan the text to find other evidence about the author.
- Ask the children to say how important the illustrations were in helping them to locate the information.

Further reading activities

- Ask the children to look through the text and find two sets of instructions ('Water' on page 22, 'Yardstick' on page 23).
- Ask them to read the instructions to a partner and discuss which are the easiest for them to follow.
- Check that the children have read and understood the instructions.

Speaking and listening activities

- Ask the children to work with a partner and collaborate to find South, using the instructions from page 23.
- Ask the children to describe what they did and how successful they were.

ICT links

- Research further information on survival and survival techniques at www.raymears.com *and* www.bearclawbushcraft.co.uk *and* www.edexcel-international.org/VirtualContent/72561.pdf
Researching information on specific climates and environments, such as this website on deserts, can by used for both building on survival knowledge and in consolidating dictionary and reference skills through children producing their own A-Z of Deserts or Cold Climates. www.oxfam.org.uk/coolplanet/ontheline/explore/nature/deserts

Writing

- Ask the children to use the text to find information and to make notes about survival in either a desert, a jungle, or frozen wasteland.
- Ask them to use their notes to write their own guide to survival in their chosen location.

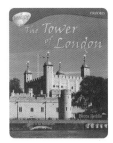

The Tower of London

Reading the book with individuals and guided reading groups

Introducing the book

- Look together at the cover. Ask the children to suggest what sort of book this is, i.e. is it fiction or non-fiction?
- Ask them to look for clues on the cover that tell what type of book it is.
- Ask the children what they already know about the Tower of London. Jot down their suggestions on the board.
- Read the Contents list together. Ask the children what they would like to find out by reading this book, and list their responses.
- Ask the children to flick quickly through the pages and notice the structure and layout of the text.
- Ask them to find an example of the use of headings, dates and captioned illustrations and photographs.

Strategy Check

- Remind the children about the strategies they can use when they meet a new word, or are unsure of the sense of a sentence.
- Ask the children to read the last entry on the Contents page, and remind them of the purpose of a Glossary. Ask them to turn to the page and read the words and their definitions together.

Focus of reading

- Explain that you want the children to find three new pieces of information about the Tower that they think will interest other readers. Ask them to note down the information, and also how they located these facts. Tell them that, after reading, you want them to read their new information to the others in the group or class, and explain how they found them.

Independent reading

- Observe the strategies the children use when they meet new vocabulary, and prompt them as needed.
- Notice when the children use the Contents page or Index to go straight to the chapters where they think the information they want will be found.

Return and respond to the text

- Ask one of the children to read their notes of new information, and to describe how they found their facts.
- Ask the other children to find the facts in the text.
- Praise the children who made use of the Contents page.
- Praise children when they demonstrate scanning the text to locate specific words or details.
- Ask other children to read their new information to the others.
- Ask the children to say which one new fact they think is the most interesting or strange.

Further reading activities

- Refer the children to the list of what they would like to find out.
- Ask them to choose three things from the list, to find the information and make a note of the answers.

Speaking and listening activities

- Ask the children to read the information about the Yeoman Warders on page 23.
- Ask them to imagine they are Beefeaters and to describe what they would tell a visitor about the Tower.

ICT links

- Research further information on http://www.tower-of-london.com

Writing

- Ask the children to use the information on pages 6 and 7 to write instructions for a guide book to the Tower of London, i.e. where to enter, what to see first, where to go next.
- Ask them to include one interesting fact to tempt visitors to the different parts of the tower.

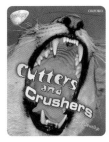

Cutters and Crushers

Reading the book with individuals and guided reading groups

Introducing the book

- Look at the cover. Ask the children to suggest what sort of book this is, i.e. is it fiction or non-fiction?
- Ask them to look for clues on the cover that tell what type of book it is.
- Ask the children to suggest what they will find out by reading the book. Jot down their suggestions on the board.
- Read the contents list together. Ask the children what they already know about some of the headings.
- Ask the children to flick quickly through the pages and look at the structure and layout of the text, noticing the use of headings, captions and fact boxes.
- Ask them to turn to page 7 and point out the heading 'Case study'. Ask them to say what a case study is, and explain if needed.
- Ask the children to locate the Index. Identify new vocabulary and discuss how to find out the meanings of the words. Demonstrate how to locate the information in the text using 'carnassial'.

Strategy Check

- Ask or remind the children about the strategies they can use when they meet a new word, or are unsure of the sense of a sentence.
- Remind the children of the purpose of a Glossary, and remind them to use the Glossary to help them understand their reading.

Focus of reading

- Explain that you want the children to find out three facts about 'herbivores', 'carnivores' and 'piscivores'. Ask them to note down the information. Tell them that, after reading, you want them to read their new information to the others in the group or class, and explain how they found them.

Independent reading

- Observe the strategies the children use when they meet new vocabulary, and prompt them as needed.
- Praise children who use the Index to go straight to the chapters where the information they want will be found.

Return and respond to the text

- Ask one of the children to read their notes about one of the headings, and to describe how they found their facts.
- Ask the other children to find the facts in the text.
- Repeat the activity with each of the other headings.
- Praise children when they demonstrate scanning the text to locate specific words or details.
- Ask the children to say which of the new facts they think is the most interesting or strange.

Further reading activities

- Ask the children to read the case studies in the text.
- Ask them to suggest why the author included case studies in the information and how they help them understand the information.

Speaking and listening activities

- Provide small mirrors for the children and ask them to look at their own teeth. Ask them to count how many teeth they have, and name the different kinds.
- Ask them to discuss the importance of their teeth and how to look after them.
- Ask them to discuss their pets' teeth, and what different types of teeth they have for eating their particular food.

ICT links

- Research further information about teeth on these websites: www.bbc.co.uk/schools/scienceclips/ages7_8/teeth_eating.shtml; www.cornwall.nhs.uk/teethonline/primary.htm; www.provet.co.uk/petfacts/healthtips/teethspecies.htm.

Writing

- Ask the children to look through the text and collect three strange or unusual facts about teeth.
- Ask them to draw an illustration and write a short paragraph or caption for their picture, and to label it.
- Collect the children's facts together for a class book.

War Children

Reading the book with individuals and guided reading groups

Introducing the book

- Look at the cover. Ask the children to suggest what sort of book this is, i.e. is it fiction or non-fiction?
- Ask them to suggest what they might find out by reading the book.
- Look together at the Contents page and ask them if this confirms their ideas about the book.
- Ask the children if they know the meaning of 'Holocaust', and where to look in the text to find definitions of new words.
- Ask the children to turn to the Glossary, and together, read the words and their definitions.
- Ask them to suggest how the War Children's lives might be different from their own lives today.

Strategy Check

- Remind the children about strategies to use when they meet new words. Ask them to re-read sentences where necessary to check for sense.

Focus of reading

- Ask the children to read pages 4 to 7, and then, with a partner, to use the Contents page and the index to find information about how children's lives were different during the War.
- Ask them to note three facts about food, school and play.
- Write the headings 'Food', 'School' and 'Play' on the board for reference.

Independent reading

- Observe children who cooperate with their partner and share their strategies for locating information.
- Praise children when they demonstrate the use of appropriate strategies for making sense of their reading, e.g. using their knowledge of familiar spelling patterns, checking the illustrations, labels and captions to help them understand the text.

Return and respond to the text

- Ask the children what they learned. Ask them if the text helped them understand how life might be different for children.
- Allow the children to refer to their notes and describe the information they found about food, school and play.
- Ask them to describe the ways in which they located the information.
- Discuss whether they can dip into the text, or if this text is better read in sequence.

Further reading activities

- Ask the children to choose another subject from the list of Contents and read the pages independently.
- Ask some of them to tell the others what they found interesting on these pages.

Speaking and listening activities

- Read together the chapter 'Evacuation' on pages 8 and 9.
- Discuss how the evacuees might feel before they were sent away.
- Ask some children to sit in the 'hot seat' and imagine they are being sent to the countryside, or to Canada, and describe how they feel and their expectations.
- Encourage other children to ask them questions.
- Ask the children if they know anyone who lived through the Second World War. Encourage them to listen to older people's experiences and recounts of what life was like then.
- Consider inviting a speaker to the school to recount what life was like as a child during the Second World War.

ICT links

- Research further information on www.bbc.co.uk/history/ww2children
- Read real memories of children in the Second World War on www.wartime-memories.fsnet.co.uk/children5.html

Writing

- Refer the children to page 19 'Help from schools'.
- Ask them to write a letter to accompany a gift of a knitted scarf for a sailor at war.
- Encourage the children to keep a fictional diary for a week of what daily life was like for a child of their age living in their town or village.

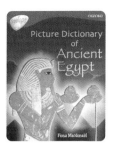

Picture Dictionary of Ancient Egypt

Reading the book with individuals and guided reading groups

Introducing the book

- Look at the cover. Ask the children to suggest what sort of book this is, i.e. is it fiction or non-fiction?
- Ask them what clues there are on the cover and in the title that tell them what they might find out by reading the book.
- Look together at the Contents page and ask them if this confirms their ideas about the book.
- Ask the children what they think a picture dictionary is. Point out its similarity to an encyclopaedia.
- Ask the children to name some typical non-fiction features they expect to find in an encyclopaedia.
- Together, read pages 4 and 5. Ask the children about the purpose of the brackets beneath some of the headwords. Read the words aloud together.
- Discuss the reason for words in italic print, and model how to use them as cross-references.

Strategy Check

- Remind the children about strategies to use when they meet new words. Ask them to re-read sentences where necessary to check for sense.
- Remind the children that reference texts can be dipped into for specific information and do not need to be read in sequence.

Focus of reading

- Ask the children to read the Contents page and make a note of six familiar words, i.e. words they know from their own experience.
- Ask them to find these headings in the text, and to read and note any new information they find.
- Explain that they will tell the others in the group about the information, the strategies they used, and which non-fiction features helped them find and understand the information.

Independent reading

- Observe children who use their alphabetic knowledge to find the headings quickly.
- Praise children when they demonstrate the use of appropriate strategies for making sense of their reading, e.g. using their knowledge of familiar spelling patterns, checking the illustrations, labels and captions to help them understand the text, and using relevant alphabetic skills.

Return and respond to the text

- Ask individual children to say which words they chose and to describe any other information they found while looking up the words.
- Ask them to describe the ways in which they located the information.
- Ask the children to say how easy it was to find information in this text. Can they name non-fiction features that helped them, e.g. illustrations, labels and captions, cross-references?

Further reading activities

- Ask the children to choose other headings from the list of Contents that they are unfamiliar with and to find and read the entries in the text.
- Ask some of them to tell the others what they found out, and the strategies they used.

Speaking and listening activities

- Discuss the purpose of an encyclopaedia or picture dictionary with the children.
- Ask the children to suggest how they could find out further information about specific headings from *Picture Dictionary of Ancient Egypt*.
- Ask them to work in small groups and plan how they would collect more information about, e.g. Cleopatra, or Tutankhamun.
- Encourage the children to collaborate in making decisions and dividing the research.
- Ask them to describe what they would do and how they would do it.

ICT links

- Research further information on:
  www.ancientegypt.co.uk;
  www.bbc.co.uk/history/ancient/egyptians.

Writing

- Discuss the structure and layout of encyclopedic texts with the children.
- Compare with other similar texts and visual dictionaries that are in the classroom.
- Explain that they are going to work in small groups and write an 'Encyclopedia of Egyptian Gods'.
- Ask them to make notes about all the gods featured in their encyclopedia.
- Ask them to work as a group, and share the information between them, each writing their share of the information using the layout and structure of the text as a model.
- Collect their writing to make an alphabetic reference text.

Links to other TreeTops and OUP titles

Oxford Literacy Web Non-Fiction KS2 for Years 3 and 4
ORT True Stories Stage 11
TreeTops True Stories Stage 11
Jackdaws Anthologies Stages 10–11
Fireflies Non-Fiction Stage 10

TreeTops non-fiction Stage 11	Treetops and OUP titles with similar subjects/themes
Wall Soldier	*Roman Britain* from Oxford Connections Year 3 *Rome* by Stephen Biesty (History) see www.oup.com/uk/children/rome
A-Z of Survival	*Kelly the Rescue Dog, Antarctic Adventure* and *Whitemen* from Treetops True Stories *Living on the Edge* and *Shackleton the Survivor* from Web Weavers *Arctic Hero* from ORT True Stories
Tower of London	*Fire! Fire*! from cross-curricular Jackdaws
Cutters and Crushers	*The Victorian Dentist, Tooth Talk* and *Sam's Tooth* from Web Spiders (Year 3/P4) *Animals* from Web Spiders (Year 4/P5)
War Children	*Eva* and *War Record* from Web Spinners *Children in World War Two* from Oxford Connections *What Was It Like?* Stage 8 ORT
Picture Dictionary of Ancient Egypt	*Mummies, Tombs and the Afterlife* from Web Weavers Year 3/P4 *Tomb Raiders* from Treetops True Stories *Egyptian Adventure* Stage 8 ORT Cleopatra from *What's Their Story*, Branch Library *Tombs and Treasure* from Web Spiders

OXFORD
UNIVERSITY PRESS

Great Clarendon Street, Oxford OX2 6DP

Oxford University Press is a department of the University of Oxford. It furthers the University's objective of excellence in research, scholarship, and education by publishing worldwide in

Oxford New York

Auckland Cape Town Dar es Salaam Hong Kong Karachi Kuala Lumpur Madrid Melbourne Mexico City Nairobi New Delhi Shanghai Taipei Toronto

With offices in

Argentina Austria Brazil Chile Czech Republic France Greece Guatemala Hungary Italy Japan Poland Portugal Singapore South Korea Switzerland Thailand Turkey Ukraine Vietnam

Oxford is a registered trade mark of Oxford University Press in the UK and in certain other countries

© Oxford University Press 2003

The moral rights of the author have been asserted

Database right Oxford University Press (maker)

First published 2003

British Library Cataloguing in Publication Data

Data available

Teacher's Notes: ISBN 978-0-19-919859-7

10 9 8 7 6

Page make-up by Fakenham Photosetting Ltd, Fakenham, Norfolk

Printed in China by Imago